Amazing Grace

Amazing Grace
Copyright ©1999 by Zondervan Publishing House

ISBN 0-310-97747-9

Requests for information should be addressed to:

Zondervan Publishing House
Mail Drop B20
Grand Rapids, Michigan 49530
http://www.zondervan.com

Senior Editor: Gwen Ellis.
Compiler: Judith Couchman.
Designer: Steve Diggs & Friends.

Printed in China

99 00 01 02 03/HK/5 4 3 2 1

Dedicated To:

From:

Date:

Contents

Introduction

Does God really love us forever? Not just when our shoes are shined and our hair is fixed. We want to know, "How does God feel about me?" That's the question. That's the concern.

Can anything separate us from the love Christ has for us? From his grace toward us? From his grace toward us? God answered our question before we asked it. So we'd see his answer, he lit the sky with a star. So we'd hear it, he filled the night with a choir; and so we'd believe it, he did what no man had ever dreamed. He became flesh and lived among us.

He placed his hand on the shoulder of humanity and said, "You're something special." Untethered by time, he sees us all. From the backwoods of Virginia to the business district of London; from Vikings to the astronauts, from cave dwellers to kings, from hut-builders to finger-pointers to rock-stackers, he sees us.

And he loves what he sees. Flooded by emotion, overcome by pride, the Starmaker turns to us, one by one, and says, "You are my child, I love you dearly. I'm aware that someday you'll turn from me and walk away. But I want you to know, I've already provided a way back."

And to prove it, he did something extraordinary.

Stepping from the throne, he removed his robe of light and wrapped himself in skin; pigmented, human skin. The light of the universe entered a dark, wet womb. He whom angels worship nestled himself in the placenta of a peasant, was birthed into the cold night, and then slept on cow's hay.

Mary didn't know whether to give him milk or give him praise, but she gave him both since he was, as near as she could figure, hungry and holy.

6

Joseph didn't know whether to call him Junior or Father. But in the end called him Jesus, since that's what the angel said and since he didn't have the faintest idea what to name a God he could cradle in his arms.

"Can anything make me stop loving you?" God asks. "Watch me speak your language, sleep on your earth, and feel your hurts. Behold the maker of sight and sound as he sneezes, coughs, and blows his nose. You wonder if I understand how you feel? Look into the dancing eyes of the kid in Nazareth; that's God walking to school. Ponder the toddler at Mary's table; that's God spilling his milk.

"You wonder how long my love will last? Find your answer on a splintered cross. On a craggy hill. That's me you see up there, your Maker, your God, nail-stabbed and bleeding. Covered in spit and sin-soaked. That's your sin I'm feeling. That's your death I'm saving. That's your resurrection I'm living. That's how much I love you."

"Can anything come between you and me?" asks the firstborn Son.

Hear the answer and stake your future on the triumphant words of Paul:

For I am convinced that neither death nor life, neither angels nor demons, neither the present nor the future, nor any powers, neither height nor depth, nor anything else in all creation, will be able to separate us from the love of God that is in Christ Jesus our Lord.

Max Lucado

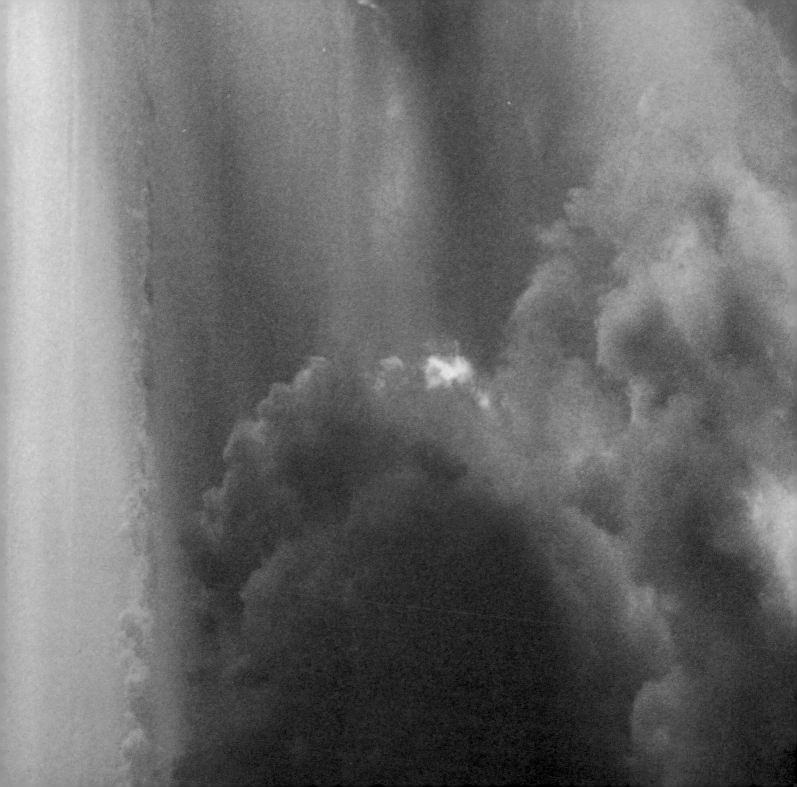

The Joy of Grace

The Joy of Grace

The greatest joy in life is to experience a genuine love relationship with God. To know that he is for us, that he loves us, is the greatest source of security any person will ever know. Discovering the glorious grace of God was one of the most important events in my whole spiritual experience. I learned to relate to God on an entirely new basis: not on the basis of my works, or of my righteousness, but on the basis of God's love for me through Jesus Christ.

That is grace, and that is what makes life worth living. In fact, it is what makes life—*real life, abundant life, fulfilling and satisfying life*— possible at all. For when our eyes are opened to the astonishing truth that our relationship with God does not depend upon the puny pebble of our own efforts but upon the massive rock of his unchanging and loving character, life opens before us in a technicolor explosion of awesome possibilities.

The Joy of Grace

Grace transforms desolate and bleak plains into rich, green pastures. It changes grit-your-teeth duty into loving, enthusiastic service. It exchanges the tears and guilt of our own failed efforts for the eternal thrill and laughter of freely offered pleasures at the right hand of God.

Grace changes everything!

Have you discovered the deep joy of living in God's grace? Would you welcome a reminder that our standing with God depends not on our own weak efforts but on what his almighty arm has accomplished for us? Wherever you are in your spiritual journey, take a few moments to consider the amazing grace of God poured out on our behalf.

Chuck Smith

11

The Joy of Grace

Happy are the simple followers of Jesus Christ who have been over-come by his grace, and are able to sing the praises of the all-sufficient grace of Christ with humbleness of heart.

Happy are those who, knowing that grace, can live in the world without being of it, who, by following Jesus Christ, are so assured of their heavenly citizenship that they are truly free to live their lives in this world.

Happy are those who know that discipleship simply means the life which springs from grace, and that grace simply means discipleship.

Happy are they who have become Christians in this sense of the word. For them the word *grace* has proved a fount of mercy.

Dietrich Bonhoeffer

Since we have been justified through faith, we have peace with God through our Lord Jesus Christ, through whom we have gained access by faith into this grace in which we now stand. And we rejoice in the hope of the glory of God. . . You see, at just the right time, when we were still powerless, Christ died for the ungodly. Very rarely will anyone die for a righteous man, though for a good man someone might possibly dare to die. But God demonstrates his own love for us in this: While we were still sinners, Christ died for us.

ROMANS 5:1-2, 6-8

13

Happy the man that finds the grace,

The blessing of our God's chosen race,

The wisdom coming from above,

The faith that sweetly works by love.

Happy beyond description he

HAPPY THE MAN THAT FINDS THE GRACE

BY CHARLES WESLEY

Who knows, the Saviour died for me,

The gift unspeakable obtains,

And heavenly understanding gains.

Wondrous Grace

Wondrous Grace

God says you are chosen. You are wanted. God desires you for his family. Today. This is the wonder of grace.

By grace we have been made alive. You were dead to God; you had awe but no one to worship; guilt but no one to forgive you; desire for purpose but no one to serve; fear but no source of hope.

This is grace for anyone who's ever despaired over sin. This is the removal of our mountain of indebtedness. If you've ever felt that gap between reality and who you're called to be, ever felt like you can't close it—this is grace for you.

God took our indebtedness and guilt and nailed it to the cross. He erased the bill, destroyed the IOU, so you are free. Unburdened. Cleansed. You can live with a heart as light as a feather. Today—no matter what you did yesterday. This is the wonder of grace.

Therefore, we can live in joy. We can have unshakable confidence—today, tomorrow, the next day, and every day through eternity. We can offer love to every human being, however ragged. This is the wonder of grace.

John Ortberg

18

God chose us in Christ before the creation of the world to be holy and blameless in his sight. In love he predestined us to be adopted as his sons through Jesus Christ, in accordance with his pleasure and will—to the praise of his glorious grace, which he has freely given us in the One he loves. In him we have redemption through his blood, the forgiveness of sins, in accordance with the riches of God's grace that he lavished on us with all wisdom and understanding.

EPHESIANS 1:4-8

19

Wondrous Grace

Son of the Blessed, what grace was manifest in your condescension! Grace brought you down from heaven; grace stripped you of your glory; grace made you poor and despicable; grace made you bear such burdens of sin, such burdens of sorrow, such burdens of God's curse as are unspeakable.

O Son of God, grace was in all your tears; grace came bubbling out of your side with your blood; grace came forth with every word of your sweet mouth; grace came out where the whips smote you; where the thorn pricked you, where the nails and spear pierced you.

O blessed Son of God, here is grace indeed! Unsearchable riches of grace! Unthought of riches of grace! Grace to make angels wonder, grace to make sinners happy, grace to astonish devils!

John Bunyan

Now we have received from God nothing but love and favor, for Christ has pledged and given us his righteousness and everything he has; he has poured out upon us all his treasures, which no man can measure and no angel can understand or fathom, for God is a glowing furnace of love, reaching even from the earth to the heavens.

Martin Luther

Monorous Grace

The power to become sons of God does not come from trying with our human will to act in a Godly manner. Our new birth comes as we are changed by the inward actions of grace.

Grace gives us the courage, strength, and boldness to let our way of seeing things and our past way of dealing with life be put to death. Grace opens the eyes of the soul to the highest holiness and beauty and transcendent wisdom of God—the way of life that is above. Then, in spirit, we learn how to live and to "walk" above every natural event—those that torment and confuse, as well as those that woo and lull us to sleep in the comforts of this world's life.

Grace is the touch and movement of God's living power within. This allows us to know that we have been reborn, and that we are adopted as His children. The life of grace far surpasses mere mental belief in the truths of God—it frees the spirit to fly powerfully above all things, with a kind of inner life that is beyond description.

John of The Cross

Blest be the wondrous grace,

That gives my soul a place

Within the mansions of Thy love!

That pardons all my sin,

And makes me pure within,

And writes my name in heaven above.

All good desires I owe,

And mercies here below,

And thoughts of grace, and hopes of heaven,

To Him, whose suffering breath

Still prayed for me in death,

Whose precious blood for me was given,

Lord, bind me to Thy sway,

And keep me every day,

Weaned from the world by Thy dear cross,

May I, redeemed by grace,

Behold Thy glorious face,

And count all other things but loss.

BLEST BE THE WONDROUS GRACE

BY GEORGE BARRELL CHEEVER AND JOSEPH EMERSON SWEETSER

The Gift of Grace

The Gift of Grace

At Calvary a man was dying who deserved hell. He was a thief. He was a murderer. Yet in the last moment he turned to Christ and said, "Lord, remember me" (Luke 23:42). In that moment Jesus turned to him and said, "Today thou shalt be with me in Paradise" (Luke 23:43).

I expect to see that man in Paradise. That man is in heaven today. Not because he could come down from the cross and be baptized. Not because he could come down from the cross and take communion. Not because he could come down from the cross and give money to charitable work. Not because he could come down from the cross and live a good life. He had been a wicked, godless man, but he was saved by the tender mercy and grace of God.

And that is what brings us to the cross. You will never understand what the cross means until you understand in your own life the assurance that God gives in his Word: "By grace are ye saved through faith; and that not of yourselves; it is the gift of God" (Ephesians 2:8).

Billy Graham

The Gift of Grace

We praise God for salvation because it is not the payment of a debt, but the gift of grace. No person enters eternal life on earth, or in heaven, as his due. It is the gift of God.

We say, "Nothing is purer than a free gift." Salvation is so purely, so absolutely a gift of God, that nothing can be more free. God gives it because he chooses to give it.

He will not barter and bargain with you. So much grace for so many tears, so much mercy for so much repentance, so much love for so many works! Salvation is not in the market except on these express terms: "Without money and without price." Freely you may be saved if you will cast out of your soul that last thought of making God your debtor.

Salvation in its entirety is a gift from God. If you will have it, there it is, complete.

Will you have it as a perfect gift?

Charles Spurgeon

27

Because of his great love for us, God, who is rich in mercy, made us alive with Christ even when we were dead in transgressions—it is by grace you have been saved. And God raised us up with Christ and seated us with him in the heavenly realms in Christ Jesus, in order that in the coming ages he might show the incomparable riches of his grace, expressed in his kindness to us in Christ Jesus. For it is by grace you have been saved, through faith—and this is not from yourselves, it is the gift of God—not by works, so that no one can boast.

EPHESIANS 2:4–9

28

There is now no condemnation for
those who are in Christ Jesus,
because through Christ Jesus the law
of the Spirit of life set me free
from the law of sin and death.

ROMANS 8:1-2

29

Marvelous grace of our loving Lord,

Grace that exceeds our sin and our guilt,

Yonder on Calvary's mount outpoured,

There where the blood of the Lamb was spilt.

Sin and despair like the sea waves cold,

Threaten the soul with infinite loss;

Grace that is greater, yes, grace untold,

Whiter than snow you may be today.

Marvelous, infinite, matchless grace,

Freely bestowed on all who believe;

You that are longing to see His face,

Will you this moment His grace receive?

Grace, grace, God's grace,

Grace that will pardon and cleanse within;

Grace, grace, God's grace,

Grace that is greater than all our sin.

GRACE GREATER THAN OUR SIN

BY JULIA J. JOHNSTON AND DANIEL B. TOWNER

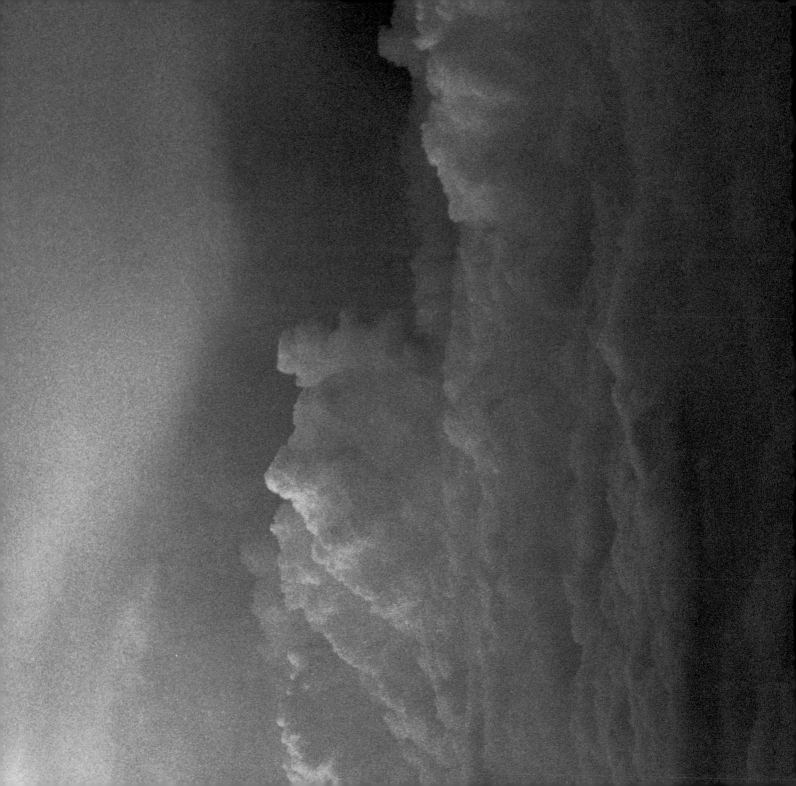

Forgiving Grace

Forgiving Grace

How do I deal with the debt I owe God?

Deny it? My conscience won't let me.

Find worse sins in others? God won't fall for that.

Claim lineage immunity? Family pride won't help.

Try to pay it off? I could, but that takes us back to the problem. We don't know the cost of sin. We don't even know how much we owe.

Then what do we do?

Simply put: The cost of your sins is more than you can pay. The gift of your God is more than you can imagine. "A person is made right with God through faith," Paul explains, "not through obeying the law" (Romans 3:28).

This may very well be the most difficult spiritual truth for us to embrace. For some reason, people accept Jesus as Lord before they accept him as Savior. It's easier to comprehend his power than his mercy. We'll celebrate the empty tomb long before we'll kneel at the cross. We, like Thomas, would die for Christ before we'd let Christ die for us.

There's not one of us who hasn't racked up more bills than we could ever pay. But there's not a one of us who must remain in debt. God has promised grace to us.

Max Lucado

Forgiving Grace

I consider myself as the most wretched of men, full of sores and corruption, and who has committed all sorts of crimes against his king; touched with a sensible regret I confess to him all my wickedness, I ask his forgiveness, I abandon myself in his hands, that he may do what he pleases with me.

This King, full of mercy and goodness, very far from chastising me, embraces me with love, makes me eat at his table, serves me with his own hands, gives me the key of his treasures; he converses and delights himself with me incessantly; in a thousand and a thousand ways, and treats me in all respects as his favourite. It is thus I consider myself from time to time in his holy presence.

Brother Lawrence

Plenteous grace with Thee is found,
Grace to cover all my sin;
Let the healing streams abound;
Make and keep me pure within.

Charles Wesley

35

All need to be made right with
God by his grace, which is a free gift.
They need to be made free from
sin through Jesus Christ. God gave
him as a way to forgive sin through
faith in the blood of Jesus.

ROMANS 3:24–25, NCV

36

If we claim to be without sin,
we deceive ourselves
and the truth is not in us.
If we confess our sins,
God is faithful and just and
will forgive us our sins and
purify us from all unrighteousness.

1 JOHN 1:8

'Twas grace that wrote my name

In life's eternal book;

'Twas grace that gave me to the Lamb,

Who all my sorrows took.

Grace taught my wand'ring feet

To tread the heav'nly road;

And new supplies each hour I meet,

While pressing on to God.

Grace taught my soul to pray,

And made mine eyes o'erflow.

'Twas grace which kept me to this day,

And will not let me go.

Saved by grace alone!

This is all my plea:

Jesus died for all mankind,

And Jesus died for me.

GRACE! 'TIS A CHARMING SOUND

BY PHILIP DODDRIDGE, AUGUSTUS M. TOPLADY, AND IRA D. SANKEY

Life~Changing Grace

Life-Changing Grace

In 1736, eleven-year-old John Newton went to sea on his father's ship, beginning a life of rebellion and immorality. He often worked on slave ships, helping to sell slaves to wealthy landowners. An ambitious young man, Newton soon owned a slave ship and was proud of his place in a bloody and cruel industry.

Only when his ship ran into a horrible storm and he feared for his life did he turn to God. In desperation he read a devotional about Christ. Newton came face-to-face for the first time with Jesus' sacrificial love, and it changed his life. He eventually renounced the evil slave trade and became a powerful and bold minister.

Years later, for his small congregation to sing, Newton penned the words to "Amazing Grace," the moving story of his conversion. Newton realized that no crime is too big, no deed is too horrible, no thought is too wicked for Christ to forgive. Christ's amazing grace covers all sin. When you accept his payment on the cross for your sin and make him Lord of your life, you are cleansed completely. Past failures no longer have a hold on your life. God washes old things away and makes you a new creation.

Charles Stanley

42

If the many died by the trespass of

the one man, how much more did

God's grace and the gift that came

by the grace of the one man,

Jesus Christ, overflow to the many.

ROMANS 5:15

Righteousness from God comes through faith in Jesus Christ to all who believe.

There is no difference, for all have sinned and fall short of the glory of God, and are justified freely by his grace through the redemption that came by Christ Jesus.

ROMANS 3:22-24

44

If anyone is in Christ, he is
a new creation; the old has
gone, the new has come!

2 CORINTHIANS 5:17

45

Amazing grace, how sweet the sound,

That saved a wretch like me!

I once was lost, but now am found,

Was blind, but now I see.

'Twas grace that taught my heart to fear,

And grace my fears relieved;

How precious did that grace appear

The hour I first believed!

Through many dangers, toils, and snares,

I have already come;

'Tis grace has brought me safe thus far,

46

And grace will lead me home.
The Lord has promised good to me,
His word my hope secures;
He will my shield and portion be

As long as life endures.
When we've been there ten thousand years,
Bright shining as the sun,
We've no less days to sing God's praise
Than when we'd first begun.

AMAZING GRACE

JOHN NEWTON

Liberating Grace

Liberating Grace

Believing in God's liberating love elevates our hearts, bringing joy in any circumstance. It fortifies us, making us invulnerable to any threat.

Do we compare ourselves with others, face or fear disapproval, become discouraged at our weakness and sins? Our loving King is not comparing. He delights in each of us; he enjoys us. He does not condemn, blame, or exclude any of us. His favor is constant. It neither increases when we excel nor lessens when we fail. It shines into our lives as we let it in.

Why do anxieties keep us awake at night? Why do we ever waste time blaming others, reproaching ourselves, thinking of excuses? These are symptoms of unbelief—of relying on something other than God's grace.

This is what happens: We need favor, and if we do not consciously receive approval from God, we automatically resort to seeking it from people. We try to prove to ourselves and to others that we are

Liberating Grace

"somebody," that we are attractive, desirable, competent, trustworthy. But we meet a frown here or a rebuke there, and discomfort sets in. We try worldly remedies. We worry, we attempt to change others, try to improve ourselves. We even pray. But any relief we get is temporary because we're dealing with symptoms. The cause—not believing God, not relying on his grace—goes unrecognized.

The remedy? Grace—God's unmerited favor, his unfailing kindness. His undeserved working on our behalf. We confess our sins and let his Word assure us of our forgiveness and adequacy in his Son. The Holy Spirit performs his therapy, dealing with the cause, healing from within. God's grace cures our inner sickness—and frequent doses will minimize recurrences.

Ruth Myers

Liberating Grace

What in the world has happened to grace? Where is the abundant life Christ offered? Are freed people supposed to live a frightened existence? Are we emancipated or not? If so, let's live like it! This isn't heresy, it's the healthiest kind of theology imaginable.

I can assure you, your old master doesn't want you to read this or think like this. He wants you to exist in the shack of ignorance, clothed in the rags of guilt and shame, and afraid of him and his whip. Like the cruel slave owner, he wants you to think you "gotta take a beatin' every now 'n' then" just so you will stay in line. Listen to me today: *That* is heresy.

Because our Savior has set us free from the old master—the supreme grace killer—he has no right whatsoever to put a whip to your back. Those days have ended, my friend. You're free.

Charles Swindoll

Now that you have been set free from sin and have become slaves to God, the benefit you reap leads to holiness, and the result is eternal life. For the wages of sin is death, but the gift of God is eternal life in Christ Jesus our Lord.

ROMANS 6:22-23

Wonderful grace of Jesus,

Greater than all my sin.

How shall my tongue describe it?

Where shall its praise begin?

Taking away my burden,

Setting my spirit free;

For the wonderful grace of Jesus reaches me.

Wonderful grace of Jesus,

Reaching to all the lost.

By it I have been pardoned,

Saved to the uttermost.

Chains have been torn asunder,

WONDERFUL GRACE OF JESUS

BY HOLDER LILLENAS

Wonderful grace of Jesus,
Greater than all my sin;

Giving me liberty;

For the wonderful grace of Jesus reaches me.

Wonderful grace of Jesus,

Reaching the most defiled.

By its transforming power

Making him God's dear child.

Purchasing peace and heaven

For all eternity;

For the wonderful grace of Jesus reaches me.

Living by Grace

Living by Grace

Grace is something you can never get but can only be given. There's no way to earn it or deserve it or bring it about any more than you can deserve the taste of raspberries and cream or earn good looks or bring about your own birth.

A good sleep is grace and so are good dreams. The smell of rain is grace. Somebody loving you is grace. Loving somebody is grace. Have you ever *tried* to love somebody?

A crucial eccentricity of the Christian faith is the assertion that people are saved by grace. There's nothing *you* have to do. There's nothing you *have* to do. There's nothing you have to *do*.

The grace of God means something like: Here is your life. You might never have been, but you are because the party wouldn't have been complete without you. Here is the world. Beautiful and terrible things will happen. Don't be afraid. I am with you. Nothing can ever separate us. It's for you I created the universe. I love you.

Frederick Buechner

58

Living by Grace

Though it is a wonderful truth to know that we are saved by grace, it is equally wonderful to know that we live by it as well. Though we labor, just as the birds of the air labor, we do not need to grasp and grab frantically, because we have One who cares for us just as he cares for the birds of the air.

Richard J. Foster

Life is not an aimless groping. We are called. "By his grace" means that God does not look around to see who will best suit his purposes and then single them out because he is pretty sure that they will do a good job. It means that God has a capacity so large in love and purpose that he calls us in order to do something for us—to give us something. Grace.

Eugene Peterson

59

The grace of God that brings salvation has appeared to all men. It teaches us to say "No" to ungodliness and worldly passions, and to live self-controlled, upright and godly lives in this present age, while we wait for the blessed hope—the glorious appearing of our great God and Savior, Jesus Christ, who gave himself for us to redeem us from all wickedness and to purify for himself a people that are his very own, eager to do what is good.

TITUS 2:11-14

60

Living by Grace

I received a letter from an old school friend the other day. After twenty-five years of friendship, it was good to read that she is still growing in the Lord. But I was especially touched with her closing salutation, "Grow in grace." It made me think: Just how have I grown in God's grace over the last year? Is this something that can be measured?

Bishop J. C. Ryle puts it this way: "When I speak of a person growing in grace, I mean simply this—that his sense of sin is becoming deeper, his faith stronger, his hope brighter, his love more extensive, and his spiritual-mindedness more marked. He feels more of the power of godliness in his heart. He manifests more of it in his life. He goes on from strength to strength, from faith to faith, and from grace to grace."

Is your sense of sin deeper than it was last year? Is your hope brighter? Do you sense more of the power of godliness in your heart?

We can be transformed into his likeness; something fundamentally different can happen in our lives from year to year. Change is possible, and a new and improved you is within reach. This is how it happens. Behold the Lord's glory and you will grow in grace.

Joni Eareckson Tada

61

Come, Thou Fount of every blessing,

Tune my heart to sing Thy grace;

Streams of mercy, never ceasing,

Call for songs of loudest praise.

Teach me some melodious sonnet,

Sung by flaming tongues above;

Praise the mount! I'm fixed upon it,

Mount of God's unchanging love!

O, to grace how great a debtor

COME, THOU FOUNT OF EVERY BLESSING

BY ROBERT ROBINSON AND JOHN WYETH

Daily I'm constrained to be!
Let Thy grace, Lord, like a fetter,
Bind my wand'ring heart to Thee.
Prone to wander, Lord I feel it,
Prone to leave the God I love;
Here's my heart, Lord, take and seal it,
Seal it for Thy courts above.

Giving Away Grace

Giving Away Grace

Our freedom from sin allows us to serve others. Before, all our serving was for our benefit, a means to somehow get right with God. Only because the grace of God has been showered upon us are we enabled to give that same grace to others. Luther expresses this thesis in his famous paradox: "A Christian is a perfectly free lord of all, subject to none. A Christian is a perfectly dutiful servant of all, subject to all."

Through the grace of God alone, and not by any work of righteousness on our part, we come into the glorious liberty of the gospel. We are all lords and kings and priests, as Luther put it. We are set free from the law of sin and death.

But this freedom is not for our sake alone—it is also a freedom to serve others. Until we are righteous we cannot really do righteous deeds no matter how hard we try. Luther said, "Good works do not make a good man, but a goodless man does good works."

Once the grace of God has broken into our lives, we are free. When we are free from the control of our neighbor, we are able to obey God. And as we obey God with a single heart, we are given a new power and desire to serve our neighbor, from whom we are now free.

Richard J. Foster

Giving Away Grace

Philip Yancey

Most ethicists would agree with the philosopher Immanuel Kant, who argued that a person should be forgiven only if he deserves it. But the very word *forgive* contains the word *give* (just as the word *pardon* contains *donum*, or *gift*). Like grace, forgiveness has about it the maddening quality of being undeserved, unmerited, unfair.

The Gospels give a straightforward answer to why God asks us to forgive: because that is what God is like. When Jesus first gave that command, "Love your enemies," he added the rationale, "that you may be sons of your Father in heaven. He causes his sun to rise on the evil and the good, and sends rain on the righteous and the unrighteous."

Anyone, said Jesus, can love friends and family: "Do not even pagans do that?" Sons and daughters of the Father are called to a higher law, in order to resemble the forgiving Father. We are called to be like God, to bear God's family likeness.

The gospel of grace begins and ends with forgiveness. And people write songs with titles like "Amazing Grace" for one reason: Grace is the only force in the universe powerful enough to break the chains that enslave generations. Grace alone melts ungrace.

Above all, love each other deeply, because

love covers over a multitude of sins. . .

Each one should use whatever gift he

has received to serve others, faithfully

administering God's grace in its various forms.

1 PETER 4:8, 10

Be merciful, just as your Father is merciful. Do not judge, and you will not be judged. Do not condemn, and you will not be condemned. Forgive, and you will be forgiven. Give, and it will be given to you. A good measure, pressed down, shaken together and running over, will be poured into your lap. For with the measure you use, it will be measured to you.

LUKE 6:36-38

69

God of grace and God of glory,
On Thy people pour Thy pow'r.

Crown Thine ancient Church's story;

Bring her bud to glorious flow'r.

Grant us wisdom; grant us courage

For the facing of this hour,

For the facing of this hour.

Lo! The hosts of evil round us

Scorn Thy Christ, assail His ways!

From the fears that long have bound us,

Free our hearts to faith and praise.

Grant us wisdom; Grant us courage

For the living of these days,

For the living of these days.

Set our feet on lofty places;

Gird our lives that they may be

Armored with all Christlike graces

In the fight to set men free.

Grant us wisdom; grant us courage

That we fail nor man nor Thee,

That we fail not man nor Thee.

"GOD OF GRACE AND GLORY"

BY HARRY EMERSON FOSDICK

71

Sufficient Grace

Before we learn the sufficiency of God's grace, we must learn the insufficiency of ourselves. The more we see our sinfulness, the more we appreciate grace in its basic meaning of God's undeserved favor. In a similar manner, the more we see our frailty, weakness, and dependence, the more we appreciate God's grace in its dimension of his divine assistance. Just as grace shines more brilliantly against the dark background of our sin, so it also shines more brilliantly against the background of our human weakness.

God equates his grace with his power as specifically displayed in our weakness. The power infusing our weakness is a concrete expression of his grace. His power comes to our aid through the ministry of the Holy Spirit in our lives. This is the mysterious operation of the Holy Spirit on our human spirit through which he strengthens us and enables us to meet in a godly fashion whatever circumstances we encounter.

Jerry Bridges

Sufficient Grace

O most blessed grace, which makes the poor in spirit rich in virtues, which renders him who is rich in many good things humble of heart, come, descend upon me, fill me quickly with your consolation lest my soul faint with weariness and dryness of mind.

Let me find grace in Your sight, I beg, Lord, for Your grace is enough for me, even though I obtain none of the things which nature desires. If I am tempted and afflicted with many tribulations, I will fear no evil while Your grace is with me. This is my strength. This will give me counsel and help. This is more powerful than all my enemies, and wiser than all the wise. This is the mistress of truth, the teacher of discipline, the light of the heart, the consoler of anguish, the banisher of sorrow, the expeller of fear, the nourisher of devotion, the producer of tears. What am I without grace, but a dead wood, a useless branch, fit only to be cast away? Let Your grace, therefore, go before me and follow me, O Lord, and make me always intent on good works, through Jesus Christ, Your Son. Amen.

Thomas à Kempis

The Lord said to me, "My grace is sufficient for you, for my power is made perfect in weakness." Therefore I will boast all the more gladly about my weaknesses, so that Christ's power may rest on me. That is why, for Christ's sake, I delight in weaknesses, in insults, in hardships, in persecutions, in difficulties. For when I am weak, then I am strong.

2 CORINTHIANS 12:9-10

76

We do not have a high priest who is unable to sympathize with our weaknesses, but we have one who has been tempted in every way, just as we are— yet was without sin. Let us then approach the throne of grace with confidence, so that we may receive mercy and find grace to help us in our time of need.

HEBREWS 4:15-16

77

He giveth more grace when the burdens grow greater;

He sendeth more grace when the labours increase;

To added afflictions he addeth his mercy,

To multiplied trials, his multiplied peace.

When we have exhausted our store of endurance,

When our strength has failed ere the day is half done;

When we reach the end of our hoarded resources,

HE GIVETH MORE GRACE

BY ANNIE JOHNSON FLINT

Our Father's full giving is only begun.

His love has no limits, his grace has no measure,

His power has no boundary known unto men;

For out of his infinite riches in Jesus,

He giveth, and giveth, and giveth again.

Grace Upon Grace

Grace Upon Grace

I've grown to see grace on its own as part and parcel of our incredible Lord. His grace saved me. His grace sustains my life. His grace showers rain and sun on the good and the evil. His grace withholds judgment on nations. Inexplicable, his grace. But I accept it and live on.

But grace upon grace? I'm floored. What can I say? His grace upon grace not only lets me live, his grace lets me serve, it lets me worship, it lets me take his name as my own, it called me by name, it grants me *fullness* of life.

His grace upon grace is too much for me. Sometimes I cry out for God to remove it because there is no way I deserve such grace. At that very moment his Spirit says, "I'm glad you see your complete dependence on me. Now, loosen your limbs. Clear your throat. I've got more work for you to do. And more grace."

Joni Eareckson Tada

Grace Upon Grace

The words "grace for grace" have been a help to me. Picture a river. Stand on its banks, and contemplate the flow of waters. A minute passes, and another. Is it the same stream still? Yes. But is it the same water? No. The liquid mass that passed you a few seconds ago now fills another section of the channel; new water has displaced it, or if you please, replaced it. *Water instead of water.*

And so hour by hour, and year by year, and century by century, the process holds: one stream, other waters—living, not stagnant, because always in the great identity there is perpetual exchange. Grace takes place of grace (and love takes the place of love); ever new, ever old, ever the same, ever fresh and young, for hour by hour, for year by year, through Christ.

Amy Carmichael

83

The Word became flesh and lived among us, and we have seen his glory, the glory as of a father's only son, full of grace and truth. (John testified to him and cried out, "This was he of whom I said, "He who comes after me ranks ahead of me because he was before me.' " From his fullness

we have all received grace upon

grace. The law indeed was given

through Moses; grace and truth

came through Jesus Christ.

JOHN 1:14–17 NRSV

Lord, thou hast promised grace for grace

To all who daily seek thy face;

To them who have, thou gives more

Out of thy vast, exhaustless store.

Each step we take but gathers strength

For further progress, till at length,

With ease the highest steps we gain,

And count the mountain but a plain.

Help us, O Lord, that we may grow

In grace as thou dost grace bestow;

And still thy richer gifts repeat

Till grace in glory is complete.

LORD, THOU HAST PROMISED

BY SAMUEL K. COX AND PETER C. LUKIN

Future Grace

The only life I have left to live is future life. The past is not in my hands to offer or alter. It is gone. Not even God will change the past. All the expectations of God are future expectations. All the possibilities of faith and love are future possibilities. And all the power that touches me with help to live in love is future power.

As precious as the bygone blessings of God may be, if he leaves me only the memory of those, and not with the promise of more, I will be undone. My hope for future goodness and future glory is future grace.

The life that's left for us to live from now to eternity will be lived by future grace, or will be lost. We are not left to ourselves, nor even to the precious memories of bygone grace. We are not left at all. Today and tomorrow and the rest of eternity "he gives a greater grace" (James 4:6).

This is not decoration on the permanent structure of the Christian life. It is what makes the Christian life permanent. We live moment by moment from the strength of future grace. If it were not there, we would perish. But it is there. And every future good that we enjoy, in this life and the next, will come from future grace.

John Piper

Future Grace

A person said to me, "Moody, if God should take your son, have you grace to bear it?" I said, "What do I want grace for? I don't want grace to bear that which has not been sent. If God should call upon me to part with my boy, He would give me strength to bear it." What we want is grace for the present, to bear the trials and temptations for every day.

Christ pays the debt and gives us enough to live on besides. He doesn't merely pay our debt—He gives us enough to live on. He gives according to our need.

Rowland Hill tells a story of a rich man and a poor man of his congregation. The rich man came to Mr. Hill with a sum of money he wished to give to the poor man and asked Mr. Hill to give it to him as he thought best, either all at once or in small amounts. Mr. Hill sent the poor man a five-pound note with the endorsement: *More to follow.*

Now, which do you think did the most good? Every few months came the remittance with the same message: *More to follow. Now that's grace. More to follow.* Yes, thank God, there is more to follow. Oh, wondrous grace!

Dwight L. Moody

All the way my Savior leads me;

What have I to ask beside?

Can I doubt His tender mercy,

Who thro' life has been my Guide?

Heav'nly peace, divinest comfort,

Here by faith in Him to dwell!

For I know, whate'er befall me,

Jesus doeth all things well.

For I know, whate'er befall me,

Jesus doeth all things well.

All the way my Savior leads me,

92

ALL THE WAY MY SAVIOR LEADS ME

BY FANNY J. CROSBY

Cheers each winding path I tread,

Gives me grace for every trial,

Feeds me with the living bread.

Tho' my weary steps may falter,

And my soul a-thirst may be,

Gushing from the Rock before me,

Lo! A spring of joy I see.

Gushing from the Rock before me,

Lo! A spring of joy I see.

Let us hold unswervingly to the hope we profess,

for he who promised is faithful. And let us

consider who we may spur one another on toward love

and good deeds. . . . let us encourage one another

—and all the more as you see the Day approaching.

HEBREWS 10:23–25

94

Grow in the grace and knowledge of our Lord and Savior Jesus Christ. To him be glory both now and forever! Amen.

2 PETER 3:18

Sources

Dietrich Bonhoeffer, *The Cost of Discipleship* (New York: Macmillan, 1963).

Jerry Bridges, *Transforming Grace* (Colorado Springs: NavPress, 1991).

Frederick Buechner, *Wishful Thinking* (New York: HarperCollins, 1993).

John Bunyan, *The Book of Jesus* edited by Calvin Miller (New York: Simon & Schuster, 1996).

Amy Carmichael, *If* (For Washington, PA: Christian Literature Crusade, n.d.).

John of the Cross, *You Set My Spirit Free* edited by David Hazard (Minneapolis: Bethany House Publishers, 1994).

Richard Foster, *Freedom of Simplicity* (SanFrancisco: HarperCollins, 1981).

Richard Foster, *The Challenge of the Disciplined Life* (SanFrancisco: HarperCollins, 1985).

Billy Graham, *Breakfast with Billy Graham* (Ann Arbor, MI: Servant Publications, 1996). Originally appeared in *Decision Magazine*, March 1994 (Minneapolis: The Billy Graham Association, March 1994).

Brother Lawrence, *The Practice of the Presence of God* (Oxford, England: OneWorld, 1993).

Max Lucado, *The Great House of God* (Nashville: Word Publishing, 1997).

Martin Luther, quoted in *Love Beyond Reason* by John Ortberg (Grand Rapids: Zondervan, 1998).

Ruth Myers, *The Perfect Love* (Colorado Springs: WaterBrook Press, 1998).

Dwight L. Moody, quoted from the sermon "Grace II" in *Glad Tidings* (New York: E. B. Treat, 1876).

John Ortberg, *Love Beyond Reason* (Grand Rapids: Zondervan, 1998).

Eugene Peterson, *Living by the Message* (SanFrancisco: HarperCollins, 1996).

John Piper, *Future Grace* (Sisters, OR: Multnomah Press, 1995).

Chuck Smith, *Why Grace Changes Everything* (Eugene, OR: Harvest House, 1994).

Charles Spurgeon, quoted from the sermon, "Grace" (Pasadena, TX: Pilgrim Publications, n.d.).

Charles Stanley, *Enter His Gates* (Nashville: Thomas Nelson, 1998).

Charles Swindoll, *The Grace Awakening* (Nashville: Word Publishing, 1996).

Joni Eareckson Tada, *Diamonds in the Dust* (Grand Rapids: Zondervan, 1997).

Mother Teresa, *A Gift for God* (SanFrancisco: HarperCollins, 1996).

Charles Wesley, from the hymn "Jesus, Lover of My Soul", 1740.

Philip Yancey, *What's So Amazing About Grace?* (Grand Rapids: Zondervan, 1997).